IT'S COMING HOME

IT'S COMING HOME

Text by Jonathan Varley

Football icon throughout © vectorplus/Shutterstock.com

An Hachette UK Company
www.hachette.co.uk

Summersdale Publishers Ltd
Part of Octopus Publishing Group Limited
Carmelite House
50 Victoria Embankment
LONDON
EC4Y 0DZ
UK

www.summersdale.com

Printed and bound by CPI Group (UK) Ltd, Croydon, CR0 4YY

ISBN: 978-1-80007-640-2

Substantial discounts on bulk quantities of Summersdale books are available to corporations, professional associations and other organizations. For details contact general enquiries: telephone: +44 (0) 1243 771107 or email: enquiries@summersdale.com.

Disclaimer: All information in this book is accurate as of April 2022.

IT'S COMING
HOME

TEST YOUR
FOOTBALL
KNOWLEDGE

summersdale

Whether you're a casual football follower or a die-hard fan of "the beautiful game", this book will prove informative, humorous and sometimes provocative!

It's Coming Home is filled with stats and trivia to keep all supporters in the know, as well as puzzles that will tax even the biggest footballing brain! There are also loads of quizzes to test your friends – whether in the dressing room or down the pub.

From World Cup history to the 2021–2022 Premiership season – and beyond – this book will prove invaluable to anyone who craves footballing facts and figures.

So, if you can tell your Maldinis from your Maradonas, or your Pelés from your Platinis, this book is a winner!

ANAGRAM SCRAMBLE

To "kick off" proceedings, let's get your brain in gear with a quintet of football-related anagrams.

REEF CIKK

DIBBLER

FIFESOD

ROCREN

CORBSARS

Now let's turn to a few facts about the Fédération Internationale de Football Association (FIFA) – the governing organization of international football.

- FIFA was founded in Paris in 1904. Back then, only a handful of national teams competed with each other: Sweden, Spain, The Netherlands, France, Belgium, Switzerland, Germany and France. How things have changed! FIFA's membership currently stands at more than 210 nations, and the organization is headquartered in Zürich, Switzerland.

- Though the organization doesn't set the laws of football – that's mainly the responsibility of the International Football Association Board (IFAB) – FIFA *does* enforce the laws across its competitions.

- Up to 2022, there have been nine FIFA presidents, including Jules Rimet (1921-1954), after whom the World Cup trophy is named. The current FIFA president is Swiss-Italian Gianni Infantino.

- FIFA accepts media queries but can only respond to those written in English, German, French or Spanish!

WORLD CUP HOST NATIONS

These are all the countries that have hosted or are due to host the FIFA World Cup – and they're worth learning for any quiz football round.

2026	USA (second time), Mexico (third time) and Canada	1990	Italy (second time)
		1986	Mexico (second time)
2022	Qatar	1982	Spain
2018	Russia	1978	Argentina
2014	Brazil (second time)	1974	West Germany
		1970	Mexico
2010	South Africa	1966	England
2006	Germany (second time)	1962	Chile
		1958	Sweden
2002	Japan and South Korea	1954	Switzerland
		1950	Brazil
1998	France (second time)	1938	France
		1934	Italy
1994	USA	1930	Uruguay (first World Cup)

N.B. There were no tournaments in 1942 and 1946 due to World War Two.

STRANGE BUT TRUE ?

Goalie Sergio Goycochea was a top ball-stopper for Argentina, helping his side reach the World Cup final in 1990. What was his strange habit that developed into a good-luck charm in later matches?

1. Due to homesickness, Goycochea couldn't play before an important match without eating his mother's speciality: traditional fainás (chickpea flatbreads) with chimichurri sauce. While this ritual helped Argentina get all the way to the final, they ultimately lost out to West Germany, 1–0.

2. Because the laws dictate that players can't leave the field of play until the match ends, Goycochea needed to "relieve" himself on the pitch prior to the penalty shoot-out in the 1990 World Cup quarter-finals against Yugoslavia. Argentina won, so the goalie often repeated his weeing!

3. Footballers are often superstitious, and Goycochea was no exception. He refused to play any World Cup matches without first tying and untying his shoelaces three times. The same applied to inserting his shin pads, bought for him by his brother for his eighteenth birthday from his favourite sports shop in Buenos Aires. He used to wear the number 3 shirt because he believed it was his lucky number, despite a goalie traditionally wearing number 1.

THE LOW-DOWN ON MESSI

Lionel Andrés Messi was born in 1987 in Argentina's third-largest city, Rosario.

At the senior level, he has played for just two teams: Barcelona and Paris Saint-Germain.

When he saw a young Messi play, legendary midfielder Diego Maradona said, "I have seen the player who will inherit my place in Argentinian football, and his name is Messi." High praise, indeed!

Messi is his country's leading goalscorer, with 80 goals in 158 appearances.

His most famous nickname is *La Pulga*, meaning "the flea". This was a childhood moniker inspired by his small stature. He stands at 5' 7" which, while not being tall, is not so diminutive either.

As of February 2022, he has more than 325 million Instagram followers.

His Messi Store clothing brand is led by Ginny Hilfiger (Tommy's sister), while the Brand Manager is none other than Maria – Messi's sister.

His wealth – including endorsements – is valued at approximately $430 million.

WORD LADDER

Take a punt on this quizzical cracker! Change one letter at a time to make "punt" into the name of a well-known footballer. Good luck!

PUNT

KANE

BALLS, BALLS, BALLS

Since the first FIFA World Cup in 1930, official tournament balls have evolved in terms of materials, colour and technology. Here are the names of the balls that have been used the most times in both World Cup final and qualifying matches. Since 1970, all the balls have been made by Adidas.

2022	Al Rihla (Arabic for "journey" or "travelogue")	1970	Telstar
2018	Telstar 18	1966	Challenge 4-star (made by Slazenger)
2014	Brazuca	1962	Crack
2010	Jabulani	1958	Top Star
2006	Teamgeist	1954	Swiss World Champion
2002	Fevernova	1950	Duplo T
1998	Tricolore	1938	Allen
1994	Questra	1934	Federale 102
1990	Etrusco Unico	1930	Tiento (first half) and T-Model (second half)
1986	Azteca		
1982	Tango España		
1978	Tango		
1974	Telstar Durlast		

N.B. Some of the balls may have been used in qualifiers, and the final match balls may have more specific or different names.

CAPTAIN FANTASTICS

Can you identify the players who lifted the famous cup from the descriptions below?

1. Which defender, with more than 100 caps for his country, lifted the golden trophy after his team won the 2014 tournament?

2. Who was the famous English skipper that led the celebrations in 1966?

3. Which goalkeeper raised the trophy at the conclusion of the 1982 final?

4. ...and which goalkeeper lifted the trophy at the 2018 tournament?

5. Brazil won the FIFA World Cup in 1994. Their captain, Carlos Caetano Bledorn Verri, had the honour of lifting the trophy at the Rose Bowl in Pasadena, California. By what one-word name is he better known?

WHEN POLITICS AND A DEFENDER CLASH

Professional footballers should know the basic rules, right? Well, there was a controversy about this at the 1974 finals that has passed into World Cup folklore. In their last group match of the tournament, Zaire (now the Democratic Republic of the Congo) conceded a free kick to Brazil. As soon as the referee's whistle blew, the Brazilian team was dumbfounded when defender Mwepu Ilunga charged out of the defensive wall and booted the stationary ball as hard as he could! What *was* he thinking?

Ilunga earned a yellow card for his rush of blood to the head. Though a commentator quipped – inappropriately – that Ilunga's actions were down to "African ignorance", Ilunga later revealed that he knew exactly what he was doing – he hoped to receive a straight red card in protest against Joseph Mobutu's (Zaire's dictator) unwillingness to pay the players properly. Unfortunately for Ilunga, the move didn't quite work out.

PREMIERSHIP REACHES ITS CAPACITY

Want to know the 20 largest stadiums in the Premier League (2021–2022) season by maximum capacity? Look no further.

1. Old Trafford – 74,879
2. Tottenham Hotspur Stadium – 62,850
3. Emirates – 60,260
4. London Stadium – 60,000
5. City of Manchester (Etihad) – 55,017
6. Anfield – 53,394
7. St. James' Park – 52,354
8. Villa Park – 42,785
9. Stamford Bridge – 40,835
10. Goodison Park – 39,221
11. Elland Road – 37,890
12. St. Mary's – 32,384
13. King Power Stadium – 32, 273
14. Molineux – 32,050
15. Falmer Stadium (Amex) – 30,666
16. Carrow Road – 27,244
17. Selhurst Park – 26,074
18. Vicarage Road – 22,200
19. Turf Moor – 21,944
20. Brentford Community – 17,250

N.B. Maximum capacities sometimes vary due to extra seating provisions for concerts and other events.

VOWEL YOU'RE TALKING!

Here are the names of some famous footballers – past and present – with the vowels deleted. Take it steady, as they get harder!

DVDBCKHM

PL

ZC

NYMR

LK MDRC

LN SHRR

NDRS NST

PL MLDN

SML T

CRAZY GANG (WIMBLEDON FC)

Just as Frank Sinatra, Dean Martin and co. were nicknamed "the Rat Pack", Wimbledon FC earned a legendary nickname in the 1980s. "The Crazy Gang" tag was coined by the media in reference to the players' boisterous behaviour and general shenanigans – much of which occurred off the field.

Spearheaded by notable characters including Vinnie Jones, Dennis Wise, John Fashanu, Lawrie Sanchez and Dave Beasant, "the Crazy Gang" were renowned for their direct style of play, puerile pranks and aggression. As Fashanu stated, "What were we like to play against? We were your worst weekend."

Wimbledon's big moment came in 1988, when they beat Liverpool's "Culture Club" in the FA Cup final – not bad considering only ten years before the club had made their debut in the old Fourth Division. Crazy, indeed!

FOOTIE RIDDLES

Here are two tricky little riddles for sharp-minded fans. Can you work out who the two England ex-professional footballers are?

Footballer 1
Something hearty to eat on a cold day
Something to look at (e.g. painting, sculpture, music, etc.)
Ear decoration

Footballer 2
A quintet on each foot
The patella is found here
Plural of first male

HE SHOOTS, HE SCORES (A LOT)

Here is a list of the top goal scorers at World Cup finals matches, prior to the 2022 World Cup (minimum of ten goals scored).

Name	Country	Goals scored
Miroslav Klose	Germany	16
Ronaldo	Brazil	15
Gerd Müller	Germany	14
Just Fontaine	France	13
Pelé	Brazil	12
Jürgen Klinsmann	Germany	11
Sándor Kocsis	Hungary	11
Gabriel Batistuta	Argentina	10
Gary Lineker	England	10
Thomas Müller	Germany	10
Teófilo Cubillas	Peru	10
Grzegorz Lato	Poland	10
Helmut Rahn	Germany	10

FOOTIE TEASERS

Get your football brain into gear to "tackle" these gems.

1. In feet, what is the height of the crossbar (from the ground) of a standard football goal?

2. What is unique about the design of the Blackburn Rovers' corner flags (at their home games)?

3. As of April 2022, the Rungrado 1st of May Stadium in North Korea is the largest football stadium by maximum capacity. To the nearest 1,000, what is the venue's capacity?

4. In 2010, the Srivaddhanaprabha family became the owners of which English football club?

5. Who scored the first-ever goal in the Premier League, and for which team was he playing?

HOW DID RED AND YELLOW CARDS ORIGINATE?

The now ubiquitous red and yellow cards were the brainchild of British teacher and referee Ken Aston. In 1962, he was invited to officiate at the World Cup, where the conduct of certain players surprised him, even though he'd kept unruly children under control! Aston asked himself, is there an easy way to show everyone that a referee wants to caution or send a player off?

Fast-forward four years and Aston was driving back from Wembley following a 1966 World Cup match. Stopping at a traffic light junction at Kensington High Street, it occurred to him that the traffic light system of red–amber–green could be understood by everyone involved in world football. When our hero returned home, he shared the thought with his wife, Hilda, who quickly came up with the idea of using colour-coded cards, which she cut to fit in her husband's shirt pocket. The red and yellow card system was born!

This simple but effective method of showing everybody that a player had been cautioned or dismissed was first used in the 1970 World Cup. The same system was later adopted by many other sports. Bravo, Mr and Mrs Aston!

WORD SEARCH

Find the following words in the grid to achieve a ten-out-of-ten score. The words all relate to professional football. Good luck!

Water bottle, Jersey, Shorts, Boots, Socks, Agent, Physio, Manager, Transfer, Promotion

J	E	R	S	E	Y	Z	S	Z	T	W
A	T	Y	U	U	O	O	H	N	R	A
B	S	T	R	E	A	N	O	N	A	T
V	O	Q	W	E	R	T	R	P	N	E
W	P	O	A	T	T	E	T	H	S	R
S	O	O	T	Y	B	I	S	Y	F	B
O	A	A	C	S	W	E	R	S	E	O
C	A	S	H	K	L	E	S	I	R	T
K	O	A	G	E	N	T	I	O	X	T
S	X	B	M	W	M	K	I	I	P	L
Q	M	A	N	A	G	E	R	J	J	E
V	P	R	O	M	O	T	I	O	N	L

TOP TEN ENGLAND SKIPPERS

Leaving aside the heroic Harry Kane – as he is still earning caps (49 so far) as the current captain – which England players have worn the armband the most?

Here is a list of the most-capped England footballers in this most prestigious of duties.

1   Bobby Moore – 90 times as captain
1   Billy Wright – 90 times
3   Bryan Robson – 65 times
4   David Beckham – 59 times
5   Steven Gerrard – 38 times
6   Alan Shearer – 34 times
6   John Terry – 34 times
8   Kevin Keegan – 31 times
9   Emlyn Hughes – 23 times
10 Bob Crompton– 22 times
10 Johnny Haynes – 22 times

FAIR PLAY OR FIBBING?

Do you know the answers to the five World Cup questions below? You have a 50:50 chance for each one, as they are all "true or false". One thing's for sure: they're all tricky!

1. True or false? The 2022 FIFA World Cup in Qatar is the tournament's 22nd competition.

2. True or false? The 2022 FIFA World Cup final is planned to take place on Qatar National Day – 18 December.

3. True or false? The estimated TV viewership over the course of the entire 2006 World Cup – held in Germany – was 49 billion (about seven times Earth's population).

4. True or false? At the 1958 World Cup in Sweden, Just Fontaine scored an incredible 14 goals in six matches.

5. True or false? Manchester United was the English club that provided the most players to the World Cup finals from 1950 to 2018.

Players from all around the globe compete in the World Cup with one "goal" – to get their hands on the celebrated trophy. Here are five snippets of trivia about the trophy (or trophies).

- Since 1930, two World Cup trophies have been used: the Jules Rimet Trophy (up to 1970), and the FIFA World Cup Trophy (1974–present).

- The trophy was originally named *Victory*, and depicted Nike, the Greek goddess of... victory, of course.

- The original Jules Rimet Trophy was stolen in 1966, as security wasn't as tight as nowadays. After Football Association (FA) chairman Joe Mears received a ransom note for £15,000 signed by someone simply named "Jackson", a mongrel named Pickles soon hit the headlines. "Jackson" turned out to be former soldier Edward Betchley, who was arrested in a sting operation in Battersea Park. Betchley had a suitcase stuffed with newspaper and £5 notes, but no trophy. Pickles to the rescue! The dog's owner, David Corbett, took his faithful friend out for a walk, and Pickles got excited around Corbett's neighbour's car. On the ground was a package wrapped tightly with string. Pickles had sniffed out the trophy! Corbett collected a handsome reward… and Pickles was undoubtedly lavished with doggy treats.

- Alas, the trophy was again stolen in 1983. This time the theft occurred in the headquarters of the Brazilian Football Confederation in Rio de Janeiro. It was never found, and the incident remains one of the most notorious footballing mysteries.

- The FIFA World Cup Trophy is 36 cm (14 in.) in height and weighs just over 6 kg (13.6 lb). It is 18-carat gold, with a base of malachite (a copper carbonate hydroxide mineral with a greenish hue).

FOOTIE TEAMS WORD JIG

The names of five non-British football teams have been divided. Join the segments of letters to reveal the teams.

ONA	ICH	BAY	BOC
AJUN	CEL	MAR	MUN
SEI	RIA	IORS	LLE
ERN	PDO	SAM	BAR

N.B. Each letter segment can only be used once!

SERIOUS FOUL PLAY?

The FA recently updated its rules for the number of matches a player will be suspended after receiving a red card. The duration depends on the severity of the offence. Here are the details, as outlined in the FA's "Essential Information for Players" document for the 2021–2022 season. It applies to the Premier League, EFL Leagues, National League, Women's Super League and Women's Championship.

Sending-off offence	Automatic suspension
Spitting	6 matches
Violent conduct	3 matches
Serious foul play	3 matches
Using offensive, insulting or abusive language or gestures	2 matches
Receiving a second caution in the same match	1 match
Denying a goal or obvious goal-scoring opportunity, either by physical offence or handball	1 match

FROM ONE TO TEN

Each correct answer to this football quiz is a number from one to ten, but each number can only be used once! Easy how you go, now...

1. Up to and including the 2018 tournament, how many different countries have won the FIFA World Cup?

2. Mexico hosted the World Cup in 198...?

3. In the 2021-2022 English Premier League, how many team names begin with a vowel?

4. How many goals did Peter Schmeichel score in the Premiership?

5. The 2002 World Cup had how many host nations?

6. At the 1966 World Cup, Eusébio scored how many goals?

7. Up to and including the 2018 World Cup, how many times have Italy been crowned World Champions?

8. In yards, what is the usual distance from the penalty spot to the edge of the penalty arc (the "D")?

9. What was David Beckham's usual shirt number for Manchester United and England?

10. Up to 2021, how many times have Everton FC won the FA Cup?

A LEGEND'S GREATEST 11 PLAYERS

Sir Stanley Matthews was the definition of "legend". Nicknamed "the Wizard of the Dribble" and "the Magician", he racked up 717 senior appearances and, in 1956, was the first player to be crowned European Footballer of the Year. So, who are Sir Stanley's favourite 11 players? Here's his personal list, which he drew up for the *Book of Lists* in 1995:

1. **Johann Cruyff, Netherlands**

2. **Diego Maradona, Argentina**

3. **Alfredo Di Stefano, Spain**

4. **Garrincha, Brazil**

5. **Ferenc Puskás, Hungary**

6. **George Best, Northern Ireland**

7. **Pelé, Brazil**

8. **Eusébio, Portugal**

9. **Peter Doherty, Ireland**

10. **Tom Finney, England**

11. **Frank Swift, England**

Not a bad starting 11, eh?

ODD ONE OUT ANAGRAM

Which of the following five footie anagrams is the odd one out?
Here's a clue – the anagrams are of player names.

1. ROOKS

2. SOLEK

3. NOOLAS

4. LIZO

5. RERNEW

WORLD CUP CARDS

Ever since the card system was implemented, players have been made all too aware of the referee's decisions – whether they are deserved or not! Look at this table detailing the total cards brandished at every World Cup since 1970. Has the game become "dirtier", or is it simply that the players have gotten better at deceiving their opponents? It's worth noting that more teams (32) competed from 1998, but either way, you decide...

Year	Host	No. of yellows	No. of reds
1970	Mexico	51	0
1974	West Germany	87	5
1978	Argentina	59	3
1982	Spain	99	5
1986	Mexico	138	8
1990	Italy	168	16
1994	USA	228	15
1998	France	254	22
2002	Japan and South Korea	267	16
2006	Germany	323	28
2010	South Africa	249	16
2014	Brazil	184	10
2018	Russia	221	4

FOOTBALLING ALIASES

Below are the nicknames of some famous faces (past or present) in world football. Can you identify the player from the pet name? Some are genius! To make it a bit easier, we've given the nationality of the footballer in question.

1. "Der Kaiser" ("The Emperor") – German

2. "El Niño" – Spanish

3. "Chicharito" ("Little Pea") – Mexican

4. "Kun" – Argentine

5. "One Size" – English

6. "Duncan Disorderly" – Scottish

7. "Crazy Horse" – English

8. "El Pibe de Oro" ("The Golden Boy") – Argentine

9. "Psycho" – English

10. "Golden Balls" – English

While the 1994 USA World Cup had all the glitz and glamour you'd expect, it was also the scene of perhaps the most cringeworthy moment in the competition's history... and the most infamous penalty miss of all time. Yes, who can forget Diana Ross's pre-match antics at the opening ceremony in Chicago? But plenty of other things went wrong on or around that evening.

- The draw was made the previous year in Las Vegas, where guest Robin Williams repeatedly referred to then FIFA President Sepp Blatter as "Sepp Bladder". Mr Blatter was not amused.

- ESPN's Bob Ley described the admin side of the organization as if "Salvador Dalí could produce a state lottery".

- Months later, a poll revealed that 71 per cent of the US population were unaware that their country was hosting the most famous sporting event on the planet!

- On the day of the opening ceremony, host Oprah Winfrey fell off her podium. The megastar later said, "You can't have an embarrassing moment because anything that has happened to you has already happened to someone else. But I don't know anybody who fell in a hole at the [FIFA World Cup] in front of thousands of people and had to be carried out spread-eagle."

- Diana Ross (her song – impeccably mimed – was "I'm Coming Out") pranced about in front of thousands of fans before delivering her coup de grâce – kicking a football to the left of the goal, which had been positioned strategically in front of the singer. As the ball went wide, the goalposts collapsed, with the goalkeeper scuttling away in embarrassment.

- As Roberto Baggio missed the final penalty, allowing Brazil to win the tournament, the 1994 World Cup will be remembered for starting *and* ending with a missed penalty!

FOOTBALLING LETTERBOX

Cross out all the letters below that appear more than once. The remaining letters will then spell out a legendary centre forward. Can you find the footballer's identity?

R	E	S	I	D
G	C	O	T	W
V	B	M	I	L
G	D	S	V	M
A	E	F	U	W
F	C	T	O	B

LONG-RANGE EXPERTS

Have you ever wondered which footballers have scored the most goals in the Premier League from direct free kicks up to the start of April 2022? Well, we have the list!

Player	No. of goals
David Beckham	18
James Ward-Prowse	13
Gianfranco Zola	12
Thierry Henry	12
Lauren Robert	11
Cristiano Ronaldo	11
Sebastian Larsson	11
Ian Harte	10
Morten Gamst Pedersen	10
Nolberto Solano	9
Jamie Redknapp	9
Frank Lampard	9

STRANGE BUT TRUE

Which of these peculiar football incidents is true? In 2001, Karl Power became known for...?

1. **Punching referee Barry Deary because Power was a spectator and disagreed with one of Mr Deary's decisions.**

2. **Becoming the unofficial mascot of his local team, Aldershot Town FC, because his father was the club's chairman (Mr Power – the best name for a chairman?)**

3. **Kissing managing director Karren Brady in an "unofficial" football photo shoot.**

4. **Infiltrating the Manchester United line-up before the team's match against Bayern Munich – as a prankster, not an official player.**

5. **Streaking at the FA Cup final between Arsenal and Liverpool. He was eventually carried off the pitch in Cardiff before evading the police to streak for a second time in a local pub!**

FOOTIE SLANG

Football slang can be heard everywhere, from World Cup commentary to the touchlines of Sunday league grounds. Here's a selection of colloquial terms used in the beautiful game – and their meanings.

- "Custodian" – goalkeeper
- "Handbags" – acts of pushing and shoving without any real violence
- "Lollipop" – moving a foot over the ball quickly to bamboozle opponents; similar to a "stepover"
- "Onion bag" – the goal net
- "Prawn Sandwich Brigade" – usually corporate "fans" who know and care little about the game
- "Gaffer" – coach or manager
- "Fergie Time" – the perception that Sir Alex Ferguson was able to influence referees so that they allowed more time in extra time which would help Manchester United to score a later winner. Probably only used by non-Man Utd fans!
- "Worldy" – a goal considered to be "world class" (e.g. an overhead kick)

- "Sitter" – an easy chance at scoring, which is often considered impossible to miss

- "Screamer" – a goal of indisputable class, usually from long range

- "Parking the bus" – when a team resorts to playing ultra-defensively, with little or no intent to attack

- "Howler" – an embarrassing mistake (e.g. when a goalkeeper lets a tame shot in through his legs)

FOLLOW THE LETTERS

To solve this puzzle, start with the letter in bold. Moving one letter at a time, either vertically or horizontally, find four famous surnames of footballers – all of whom are non-British.

B	U	F	B	E	G	A
I	A	F	O	J	A	I
L	T	I	N	O	A	K
S	C	Y	E	A	H	B
T	E	M	S	L	A	O
T	W	A	R	A	S	N
E	U	D	S	M	O	N

MOST EXPENSIVE FOOTBALLERS

The table below shows the footballers who have fetched the highest transfer fees as of February 2022.

Name	Transfer	Fee
Neymar	Barcelona to Paris Saint-Germain	£198 million (2017)
Kylian Mbappé	Monaco to Paris Saint-Germain	£163 million (2018)
Antoine Griezmann	Atlético Madrid to Barcelona	£107 million (2019)
Philippe Coutinho	Liverpool to Barcelona	£105 million (2018)
João Félix	Benfica to Atlético Madrid	£104 million (2019)
Jack Grealish	Aston Villa to Manchester City	£100 million (2021)
Romelu Lukaku	Inter Milan to Chelsea	£97.5 million (2021)
Ousmane Dembélé	Borussia Dortmund to Barcelona	£97 million (2017)
Paul Pogba	Juventus to Manchester United	£89.3 million (2016)
Eden Hazard	Chelsea to Real Madrid	£89 million (2019)
Cristiano Ronaldo	Real Madrid to Juventus	£88 million (2018)
Gareth Bale	Tottenham Hotspur to Real Madrid	£85.1 million (2013)

N.B. Due to contract clauses, some of the fees are "reported" (i.e. estimated).

WHAT'S THAT SOUND?

This quiz requires a solid knowledge of World Cup locations. The following seven cities or towns have all been venues for World Cup matches – but they are each missing one letter. Find the missing letter and place it in the grid below to spell out something players and fans might hear at football matches. What's the word?

1. POLOK_ANE

2. KAS_IMA

3. REC_FE

4. LEN_

5. _OLUCA

6. BER_IN

7. _LCHE

1	2	3	4	5	6	7

Several footballers have graced both famous stadiums *and* film sets. Here are three footballers and some little-known facts about their acting careers. Enjoy!

Vinnie Jones – The hard man of football got his first break in 1998's *Lock, Stock and Two Smoking Barrels*, playing debt collector Big Chris. On his first day of filming, Jones had just been released from police custody after an altercation with a neighbour. *Snatch* and *Gone in Sixty Seconds* followed in 2000, cementing Jones's tough-guy image in Hollywood.

Pelé – Sir Michael Caine revealed he only agreed to star in 1981's *Escape to Victory* because of the Brazilian legend. On set, co-star Sylvester Stallone broke one of his fingers while trying to save one of Pelé's shots on goal.

Olivier Giroud – Okay, so plenty of other football film stars deserve a mention (Eric Cantona, Bobby Moore, etc.), but this one is pretty eye-opening. Did you know that the French ex-Arsenal and Chelsea forward has a connection with Spider-Man? Giroud voiced the Green Goblin in the French version of *Spider-Man: Into the Spider-Verse*. His Spidey senses were tingling with that role!

WHO'S THE BOSS?

Here are the surnames of five famous football managers (past and present) that have been split into groups of letters. Your job is to join the groups to reveal the five "gaffers". They are all non-British.

NHO	ER	CO	ARD
GU	TTI	ELO	WE
NTE	MOU	IO	LA
NG	ANC	RI	

N.B. Each letter segment can only be used once!

ALL-TIME WORLD CUP POINTS

Ever wondered which teams have accrued the most points at World Cups? Wonder no more with this handy table!

Team	Total points
Brazil	237
Germany	221
Italy	156
Argentina	144
France	115
England	108
Spain	105
Netherlands	93
Uruguay	84
Sweden	70
Belgium	69
Mexico	62
Yugoslavia	56
Poland	53
USSR (as Russia from 1994)	51

N.B. These stats are accurate up to and including the 2018 World Cup.

WORLD CUP RECALL

?

Answer the following three questions about the World Cup. How far back can you remember?

1. Diego Maradona's wonder goal against England in the 1986 World Cup quarter-final was the very definition of dribbling wizardry. It has gone down in history as one of the finest strikes witnessed anywhere in the world. He beat (or passed) defender Terry Butcher twice on his way to score. Name the other four English players he dribbled past.

2. Name the four German players who scored three goals or more at the 1990 World Cup.

3. Which venue hosted the 1994 World Cup final?

Rivalries in football are often fierce and long-standing, but location plays a huge part, too. Here are three conflicts that might just be too close for comfort.

1. The two closest – geographically speaking – professional football teams in the UK are Dundee FC (Dens Park) and Dundee United (Tannadice Park). The distance between the two grounds is approximately 100 m. In fact, if the two locations are entered into a well-known route-finder website, the time taken by car from one ground to the other is just 33 seconds. The website's instructions are simply: "Head south-east on Tannadice Street toward Hindmarsh Avenue. Destination will be on the left".

2. Nottingham Forest and Notts County are separated by the River Trent, and before the latter dropped into the National League, they were the two closest English clubs in the top four leagues. The route-finder website reveals the distance is an approximate 0.6-mi drive (locals may find it quicker to walk, though!).

3. Liverpool FC and Everton FC are about 0.8 mi apart, with the 110-acre Stanley Park – a public park, even though it sounds

like a football stadium – sandwiched between the two great grounds of Anfield and Goodison Park. As of the 2021–2022 season, they are the spatially closest English clubs in the top four leagues.

If you're obsessed with proximity, also check out MTK Budapest and BKV Előre SC of Hungary, and Malmö FF and IFK Malmö in Sweden!

RIDDLE ME THIS...

Below are two sets of clues. Solve the clues to reveal the names of two football teams. This requires a bit of lateral thinking, so put your brain into gear!

Clues to football team no. 1
Anne, Victoria, Elizabeth, etc.
Central, Hyde, etc.
The team who call Ibrox home

Clues to football team no. 2
Epping, New, Sherwood, etc.
Background colour of the Bangladesh flag
Doncaster, Blackburn, Tranmere, etc.

NINETEENTH-CENTURY STATS

The conventions of the modern game tend to be taken for granted, but in the nineteenth century, there were several surprising changes to the rules and regs. Let's look at them now and consider where the game would be without them.

1863   In England, the rules of Association Football are devised.

1869   Goal kicks are introduced (goalies were allowed up to 30 seconds at a time for "tactical" time wasting!).

1870   A goalkeeper's position is officially recognized.

1872   Corner kicks were first taken.

1874   Players' safety is acknowledged by the introduction of shin pads.

1875   Crossbars were added (finally).

1877   A game's duration is set to 90 minutes.

1878   Referees first used a whistle to control a football game.

1891   Back of the net! Yep, in 1891, goal nets were trialled for the first time.

1891 Penalty kicks were introduced.

1891 In the same year, a "centre referee" was
      adopted (before then, two umpires were used
      – one for each team).

WHO AM I?

Work out the identities of these two players:

1. I was born in 1976 in Görlitz. I finished runner-up in the 2002 World Cup. In the early 2000s, I was a Champions League finalist. I won league titles in both Germany and England.

2. I was born in Lancashire in the same year England won the World Cup. I scored 27 goals for England in 62 matches.

When you're a top footballer and nationally famous, you can say anything (ish). Well, here are some of Swedish superstar Zlatan Ibrahimović's most memorable or contentious quotes.

- "A World Cup without me is nothing to watch, so it is not worth waiting for the World Cup."

- "I won't be the King of Manchester – I will be the God of Manchester."

- "It's true I don't know much about the players here, but they definitely know who I am."

- "What [John] Carew does with a football, I can do with an orange."

- "Only God knows… you're talking to him now."

- "First, I went left; he did too. Then, I went right, and he did too. Then, I went left again, and he went to buy a hot dog."

- And finally: "I can't help but laugh at how perfect I am."

Who said some footballers have egos, eh?

AMUSING ANAGRAMS

The letters in the names of five famous footballers, past and present, have been cunningly jumbled up to (hopefully) comic effect. Can you work out the five names?

1. A JAM TUNA

2. AN ADORDED AMIGO

3. A LIVID GONAD

4. EVIL BRAZILIAN AFRO

5. A DWARVES DINNER

QATAR 2022 VENUES

Here are the eight venues at the 2022 World Cup, the first to be held in the Middle East, plus some bonus info thrown in for proper fans.

Stadium	Capacity	Trivia	No. of games
Lusail (Iconic) Stadium	80,000	Host venue for the final. Design pays homage to the fanar lantern	10
Al Bayt Stadium	60,000	Traditional Arab tent design	8, including the opening match
Ahmad Bin Ali Stadium	40,000	Home to the hugely popular Al-Rayyan Sports Club	7
Stadium 974	40,000	Innovative design inspired by Qatar's global trading – "974" is Qatar's international dialling code	7

Stadium	Capacity	Trivia	No. of games
Education City Stadium	40,000	Named because of the numerous universities in the stadium's vicinity	8
Al Thumama Stadium	40,000	Design inspired by the *gahfiya*, a traditional hat worn across the Middle East	8
Al Janoub Stadium	40,000	Design inspired by *dhow* boats, and the venue contains a wedding hall	7
Khalifa International Stadium	40,000	Built in 1976; previously hosted the Arabian Gulf Cup, the AFC Asian Cup and the Asian Games	8

CR7

Cristiano Ronaldo is a global superstar, but how much do you know about him? Separate the facts from the myths with these true or false statements.

1. He was born in Madeira.

2. His first goal for Manchester United was against Bolton Wanderers.

3. He moved to Real Madrid from Manchester United for (a then world record) £95 million.

4. He was the second-highest goalscorer at Euro 2020.

5. An airport is named after him.

6. As of May 2022, he had over 430 million Instagram followers.

7. In February 2022, he "tweeted" that "Football is and will always be the best thing the world has to offer."

8. He signed with Juventus in 2017.

"The most stupid, appalling, disgusting and disgraceful display of football, possibly in the history of the game."

This was how legendary commentator David Coleman described the match between Italy and hosts Chile at the 1962 World Cup in the South American country's capital city. It was dubbed the "Battle of Santiago" – with good reason.

Englishman Ken Aston (who later invented the red–yellow card system) refereed with aplomb, but he couldn't prevent the awful on-pitch behaviour that shocked the 66,000 pectators.

The first foul set the precedent – after just 12 seconds! Seven minutes later, Aston wanted to send off Italian Giorgio Ferrini for kicking an opponent. The poor ref couldn't speak Italian and, because the penalty card system hadn't been invented, the pugnacious Ferrini had to be dragged off the pitch by a combination of security guards and his own teammates. Then, just before half-time, Chilean Leonel Sánchez punched Mario David, which went unnoticed by Aston. In retaliation, David kicked Sánchez minutes later. Not finished yet, Sánchez took aim at Humberto Maschio and broke his nose with a left hook.

Perhaps Coleman was right – there's never been anything like the Battle of Santiago since.

WORD SEARCH

Find all the words below in the grid. They are all nicknames of Premier League football teams in the 2021-2022 season. The word "the" has been omitted.

Eagles, Blues, Toffees, Clarets, Seagulls, Foxes, Magpies, Hammers, Canaries, Red Devils, Villains, Gunners

E	A	G	L	E	S	V	W	E	R	B
Q	F	O	X	E	S	I	G	S	S	L
T	D	C	H	H	P	L	U	O	E	U
O	X	L	N	K	A	L	N	R	A	E
F	O	A	S	S	T	A	N	E	G	S
F	G	R	J	L	K	I	E	D	U	E
E	I	E	I	R	R	N	R	D	L	G
E	O	T	E	Q	H	S	S	E	L	C
S	G	S	A	W	X	K	E	V	S	V
E	G	P	C	A	N	A	R	I	E	S
H	A	M	M	E	R	S	K	L	K	M
M	A	G	P	I	E	S	L	S	E	N

SING IF YOU'RE PROUD

Since the '60s, World Cup-themed songs – of varying quality – have spurred England's team on to performances of varying quality. Here's a list of all the national side's official tournament songs – your age might determine how many you can remember!

Year	Song	Performers
1966	"World Cup Willie"	Lonnie Donegan
1970	"Back Home"	England squad
1982	"This Time (We'll Get It Right)"*	England squad
1986	"We've Got the Whole World at Our Feet"	England squad
1990	"World in Motion"	New Order, England squad – plus a "rap" by John Barnes
1998	"(How Does It Feel to Be) on Top of the World?"	England United (Echo and the Bunnymen, Space, Simon Fowler and the Spice Girls)
2002	"We're on the Ball"**	Ant and Dec
2006	"World at Your Feet"	Embrace
2010	[Unofficial song] "Shout (Shout for England Song)"	Dizzee Rascal feat. James Corden

Year	Song	Performers
2014	"Sport Relief's Greatest Day"	Gary Barlow plus various singers and footballers, inc. Michael Owen, Gary Lineker, etc.

* They didn't...
** They weren't...

N.B. Several other well-known songs recorded for the England team (e.g. "Three Lions") were for the Euros.

1962 – WHAT HAPPENED NEXT?

Football has a knack of being thrilling, nerve-racking and sometimes just plain amusing. It was certainly the latter at the 1962 World Cup in Chile, when England played Brazil in a quarter-final match. During the match, a dog invaded the pitch, but what happened next?

1. The dog belonged to Brazilian player Vavá, whose wife rushed onto the pitch in her "Sunday best", complete with high heels – which only hindered her progress when the dog lay down in a patch of mud!

2. A lone pigeon caught the interest of the dog, who ran after it, delaying the match by 6 minutes. The pigeon evaded the canine's chase and was eventually caught by Brazilian player Garrincha – at the time, a keen ornithologist!

3. The dog was confronted by Jimmy Greaves, resulting in the canine "relieving" itself over the England striker's shirt – literally causing a stink!

In 2021, Alan Shearer and Thierry Henry were the first two footballers to be inducted into the Premier League Hall of Fame. There were six more places up for grabs, with 23 shortlisted.

These were the 23 other players shortlisted:

- Tony Adams
- David Beckham
- Dennis Bergkamp
- Sol Campbell
- Eric Cantona
- Andy Cole
- Ashley Cole
- Didier Drogba
- Les Ferdinand
- Rio Ferdinand
- Robbie Fowler
- Steven Gerrard
- Roy Keane
- Frank Lampard
- Matt Le Tissier
- Michael Owen
- Peter Schmeichel
- Paul Scholes
- John Terry
- Robin van Persie
- Nemanja Vidić
- Patrick Vieira
- Ian Wright

And the final six that joined Messrs Shearer and Henry?

Eric Cantona, Roy Keane, David Beckham, Dennis Bergkamp, Frank Lampard and Steven Gerrard.

PUZZLING FOOTBALL TEAMS

The following are clues to some UK football teams. Can you work them out and get three out of three?

Football team 1
Famous fictional fox
Yorkshire river
Another word for "combined"

Football team 2
Surname of famous footballing brothers
Sporty, in good shape, etc.

Football team 3
Large waterfowl
Expanse of salt water
Large human settlement

TOTAL NUMBER OF GOALS SCORED AT EACH WORLD CUP

Year	Host	No. of goals scored
1930	Uruguay	70
1934	Italy	70
1938	France	84
1950	Brazil	88
1954	Switzerland	140
1958	Sweden	126
1962	Chile	89
1966	England	89
1970	Mexico	95
1974	West Germany	97
1978	Argentina	102
1982	Spain	146
1986	Mexico	132
1990	Italy	115
1994	USA	141
1998	France	171
2002	Japan and South Korea	161
2006	Germany	147
2010	South Africa	145
2014	Brazil	171
2018	Russia	169

JUMBLED-UP SURNAMES

Think this will be straightforward? We'll see…

The surnames of four famous footballers – now retired – have been cut up into small sections. Simply join the sections to reveal their names – some sections consist of just one letter to make it just that little bit more exasperating!

IO	BE	GKA	NI
I	AT	GA	NE
GG	COI	S	PL
MP	BA	R	G

Here are some facts about Argentine legend Diego Armando Maradona.

Maradona was born in 1960 in Lanús, the capital of the Lanús Partido province, greater Buenos Aires, Argentina.

As a boy, he played for local junior team Los Cebollitas, which means "the Little Onions".

At the age of 16, Maradona played for Argentinos Juniors, scoring 116 goals in five seasons.

In 1981, he moved to Boca Juniors, immediately helping them win the championship.

Barcelona was his next club for two years, after which he went to Napoli for seven years (scoring 81 goals in 188 appearances).

The 1986 tournament saw perhaps the most famous – or controversial, depending on your nationality – incident in World Cup history. Maradona's "Hand of God" goal against England in the '86 World Cup quarter-finals will never be forgotten.

Maradona passed away in November 2020 at age 60.

FOOTBALLING ANAGRAMS

Below you'll find that the letters of some famous English footballers of yesteryear have been mixed up. See how many you can correctly unravel!

1. TORJ HENRY

2. FIND NOIR READ

3. HAH ME SYRINGE DDT

4. JOBSHARE NN

5. RED DISH CLAW

THEY WON BY HOW MUCH?

To add to your (no doubt already) vast footie statistical knowledge, here are the biggest margins of victory in World Cup history.

Margin (goals)	Year	Result
9	1982	Hungary 10–1 El Salvador
9	1954	Hungary 9–0 South Korea
9	1974	Yugoslavia 9–0 Zaire
8	1938	Sweden 8–0 Cuba
8	1950	Uruguay 8–0 Bolivia
8	2002	Germany 8–0 Saudi Arabia
7	1954	Uruguay 7–0 Scotland
7	1954	Turkey 7–0 South Korea
7	1974	Poland 7–0 Haiti
7	2010	Portugal 7–0 North Korea

Honourable mentions in recent times

2014 – Germany 7–1 Brazil

2006 – Argentina 6–0 Serbia and Montenegro

FIFA ALL-STAR XI

In 2002, FIFA published a "World Cup Dream Team", as voted for by over 1.5 million fans worldwide in an online poll.

We've added each player's usual position to help you work out the team, as well as the player's initials (how they're commonly known). How many can you identify?

Position	Initials
Goalkeeper	LY
Left back, central defender	PM
Central defender	FB
Left back	RC
Attacking midfielder, second striker	RB
Attacking midfielder	ZZ
Midfield "playmaker"	MP
Attacking midfielder, second striker	DM
Striker	R
Forward, attacking midfielder	JC
Forward, attacking midfielder	P

Whether humorous, slightly strange or downright bizarre, here are some names of – past or present – football teams that will prove advantageous next time you're quizzing with footie-mad friends!

- **Joe Public FC – Trinidad and Tobago**
- **FC Santa Claus – Lapland, Finland (where else?)**
- **Miscellaneous SC – Botswana**
- **Anti Drugs Strikers FC – Sierra Leone**
- **Deportivo Morón – Argentina**
- **FL Fart – Norway**
- **4.25 Sports Club – North Korea**
- **Eleven Men in Flight FC – Eswatini (Swaziland). It's interesting to note that other Eswatini teams include Young Buffaloes, Green Mambas and… er, Manchester United**
- **Insurance Management Bears FC – Bahamas**
- **Cape Coast Mysterious Dwarfs – Ghana**
- **Botswana Meat Commission FC – Botswana (of course)**
- **Always Ready – Bolivia**
- **Chicken Inn FC – Zimbabwe**

UTTERLY QUOTABLE

Can you work out the (slightly naughty-sounding) phrase attributed to a famous football manager? We won't tell you the number of words, but the letters are in the correct order. Some letters have been deleted, as we're sure you've worked out already!

		U			K		B		M		I	M	

FAIR PLAY, REF!

Since 1970, FIFA has generated a system that rewards teams at the World Cup for general good behaviour.
  Here are some stats about the FIFA Fair Play Trophy:

- Only teams that qualify for the second round of the World Cup are considered.

- The winners of the award earn a diploma.

- Each player of the winning team also earns a fair play medal.

- The trophy-winning team is awarded $50,000 worth of football equipment for youth development.

Which leads us to the winners of this most satisfactory award:

Year	Winners
1970	Peru
1974	West Germany
1978	Argentina
1982	Brazil
1986	Brazil
1990	England
1994	Brazil
1998	England and France
2002	Belgium
2006	Brazil and Spain
2010	Spain
2014	Colombia
2018	Spain

MANAGER'S SPECIAL

?

Let's recall the starting XI of two managers' first games in charge of their new clubs. We've listed the starting teams of Mikel Arteta's Arsenal on Boxing Day 2019, and Ole Gunnar Solskjær's debut as Manchester United boss in late 2018. Which two players are missing from each line-up?

Arsenal starting XI	Manchester United starting XI
Leno	De Gea
Maitland-Niles	Young
Luiz	Jones
Papastathopoulos	Lindelof
Saka	Shaw
Xhaka	?
Torreira	Matic
Nelson	Pogba
?	Lingard
Aubameyang	Rashford
Lacazette	Martial

Fans throughout the world enjoy collecting football stickers. The leading producer, Panini, was particularly adored in the 1980s and '90s. Let's reminisce with some facts about this much-loved brand.

- Panini was founded in 1961 in Modena, a city in northern Italy a few miles north-west of Bologna.

- Today, it employs approximately 1,200 staff.

- It has subsidiaries throughout Europe, Latin America and the US.

- While footie fans associate Panini with stickers, the company also publishes children's books, comics, manga and graphic novels.

- It produces about 7,000 publications annually.

- Panini launched its first sticker album in the UK for the 1970 World Cup (52 pages, 271 stickers).

- The craze generated its own terminology, including "swapsies", "got, got, need" and "shinies".

- Panini's album for the 2014 World Cup was its most successful, with UK sales in excess of £50 million. It had 80 pages, with 640 stickers to be collected.

- "Panini" means "sandwiches" in Italian; the singular is "panino".

WORD LADDER

Here's another word quiz for football lovers. Change one letter at a time to turn the first word into the famous Italian club "Roma".

SALT

ROMA

OFF YOU GO, SON

No player should boast about being sent off, but it does happen. The England footballers below have all been shown the red card while playing for their country.

Player	Year	Opposition
Reece James	2020	Denmark
Harry Maguire	2020	Denmark
Kyle Walker	2020	Iceland
Raheem Sterling	2014	Ecuador
Steven Gerrard	2012	Ukraine
Wayne Rooney	2011	Montenegro
Rob Green	2009	Ukraine
Wayne Rooney	2006	Portugal
David Beckham	2005	Austria
Alan Smith	2002	Macedonia
David Batty	1999	Poland
Paul Scholes	1999	Sweden
Paul Ince	1998	Sweden
David Beckham	1998	Argentina
Ray Wilkins	1986	Morocco
Trevor Cherry	1977	Argentina
Alan Ball	1973	Poland
Alan Mullery	1968	Serbia and Montenegro

N.B. This includes all national matches – including friendlies – and is not confined to the World Cup.

REFERESS IN THE SPOTLIGHT

Below are two incidents that achieved fame thanks to the referee. Correctly identify the scenario from the three options.

1. In 2008, Belarus ref Sergei Shmolik hit the headlines during a league match between FC Naftan and FC Vitebsk. Why?

   a) A rather boisterous streaker invaded the pitch, stopping play by four minutes. Mr Shmolik gave chase and stopped the intruder by tackling him to the ground – removing his trousers in the process. Amazingly, Shmolik was later fined and ordered to do 100 hours' community service.

   b) Having complained of back pain, Shmolik was moving erratically throughout the game – especially the second half. After the match, tests proved that Mr Shmolik was, in fact, incredibly drunk.

   c) After a fan threw a red and green (Belarus's national colours) inflatable beach ball onto the pitch, it burst in front of Shmolik's face when he picked it up, resulting in the unfortunate ref being carried off and hospitalized. The local newspaper headline the next day read: "Ref blows up early."

2. Graham Poll was involved in a well-publicized incident during the 2006 World Cup. Why?

   a) Poll's watch stopped, so the 90 minutes plus 4 minutes stoppage time actually equated to an erroneous 101 minutes.

   b) The English ref showed the same player a yellow card three times.

   c) Poll forgot his whistle, so the start of the game was delayed by several minutes while the assistant referees combed their dressing room for the much-needed item.

George Best was considered one of the most naturally gifted footballers of all time. You didn't have to be a Manchester United or Northern Ireland fan to have been astonished by Best's skills on the pitch. Here's a short profile of the player dubbed "the Fifth Beatle".

Born in Belfast, Best spent a lot of his youth in snooker halls – despite being a talented footballer from an early age.

In 1961, Manchester United scout Bob Bishop spotted Best when the Northern Irishman was 15 years old, declaring to manager Matt Busby via a telegram: "I think I've found you a genius."

Two years later, Best made his senior debut for Manchester United in September 1963.

Best was the youngest player of a trio known as "the Holy Trinity" or "the United Trinity" – the other two being Denis Law and Bobby Charlton. They helped Manchester United become the first English club to win the European Cup in 1968, with a 4–1 victory against Benfica.

In that same season, rivals Manchester City pipped Manchester United to the domestic title. Best became good friends with City player Mike Summerbee, and together they opened a string of fashion boutiques.

Best was inducted into the English Football Hall of Fame in 2002. In the same year, he was the winner of the BBC Sports Personality of the Year Lifetime Achievement Award.

Sadly, Best passed away in November 2005 at age 59.

GLOBAL JUMBLE

We've jumbled up the letters of five non-UK football teams. Can you identify all five clubs?

1. JBOSANIRCUO

2. RNNIIEMATL

3. CFRZIESAKIEH

4. AELLLRARVI

5. YAAAAAGTRSL

WORLD CUP REGULARS

Multiple footballers have appeared at numerous World Cups. But which player has played the most matches at this most prestigious of contests? Find out below.

Player	Country	Matches played
Lothar Matthäus	Germany	25
Miroslav Klose	Germany	24
Paolo Maldini	Italy	23
Diego Maradona	Argentina	21
Uwe Seeler	Germany	21
Władysław Antoni Żmuda	Poland	21
Philipp Lahm	Germany	20
Cafu	Brazil	20
Grzegorz Lato	Poland	20
Javier Mascherano	Argentina	20
Bastian Schweinsteiger	Germany	20

N.B. Peter Shilton played in 17 World Cup games for England.

GLOBAL TEAMS

Match the teams with the cities in which they are based. Sounds simple, but some of these are tough!

Team	City
Corinthians	La Paz
River Plate	Prague
Al Ahly SC	Stockholm
Forge FC	Mexico City
The Strongest	Helsinki
FK Partizan	Cairo
AIK	Hamilton (Ontario)
Young Boys	São Paulo
Beşiktaş	Belgrade
HIFK	Buenos Aires
Bohemians Praha 1905	Bern
América	Istanbul

It was one of the most extraordinary acts seen at an English football match.

In January 1995, Crystal Palace were hosting Manchester United, when "the King of Manchester" Eric Cantona kicked out at Palace defender Richard Shaw, resulting in referee Alan Wilkie showing the fiery Frenchman a red card. "There's the morning headline!" claimed BBC commentator Clive Tyldesley. He was wrong; there was more to follow…

Leaving the pitch, the Red Devils' no. 7 reacted to a comment from Palace fan Matthew Simmons. Was there a battle of words? Maybe some finger-pointing? No. Almost unbelievably, Cantona vaulted the advertising board with a one-footed kung fu kick at Simmons, then followed up with a punch. "Oh, this is outrageous!" stated Tyldesley, clearly as shocked as all the viewers.

At the trial, Simmons claimed he had shouted, "Off! Off! Off! It's an early bath for you, Mr Cantona!" Cantona claimed that Simmons was far less civil, and that Simmons's comments were offensively xenophobic.

Later, Cantona said, "I have one regret. I didn't kick him more than that."

The game finished 1–1, by the way.

ENGLAND WORLD CUP JIG

Here are the surnames of five famous English footballers who have excelled at the World Cup – only they've been split up again. Piece the segments together to reveal the notable quintet! Each letter slice can only be used once, of course.

TON	KER	ORE	RLT
SH	VES	LI	ON
GR	MO	NE	CHA
IL	EA		

BEST PLAYERS NEVER TO HAVE WON THE PREMIER LEAGUE TITLE

The BBC trio of Gary Lineker, Alan Shearer and Micha Richards often appear on top-ten lists of Premier League footballers. Here are Shearer and Richards's lists of the best players never to have won England's top title, as shortlisted by the BBC.

Alan Shearer	**Micha Richards**
10. Stuart Pearce	10. Stuart Pearce
9. Son Heung-min	9. Matt Le Tissier
8. Matt Le Tissier	8. Robbie Fowler
7. Fernando Torres	7. Son Heung-min
6. Luis Suárez	6. Gianfranco Zola
5. Gareth Bale	5. Fernando Torres
4. Robbie Fowler	4. Gareth Bale
3. Gianfranco Zola	3. Luis Suárez
2. Harry Kane	2. Harry Kane
1. Steven Gerrard	**1. Steven Gerrard**

Do you agree with them both?

THE RIDDLER STRIKES AGAIN!

?

Here's a cunning riddle that some may guess easily... while others may struggle!

Dave bets Tim £100 that he can predict the score of the Arsenal v Everton game before it starts. Tim agrees and loses the bet. But why?

Footballers rarely go through their careers without the odd injury. But sometimes, an injury is picked up in the most bizarre circumstances. Here's a pick of them.

- After the 1993 League Cup final against Sheffield, Arsenal legend Tony Adams hoisted Steve Morrow on his shoulders in celebration... unfortunately, Adams dropped Morrow, who broke his arm and was taken to hospital.

- In 2022, Everton manager Frank Lampard declared after his side's last-minute victory against Newcastle, "I've broken my hand, by the way, in the celebrations. I'd take it for three points. It's a bit shaky, but it's fine. I don't care." Funny how a victory can dull pain!

- In the 1993–1994 season, goalkeeper Dave Beasant missed eight games for Chelsea. Was it a rash tackle, hamstring injury or illness? Nope... he dropped a 2 kg jar of salad cream on his foot. Not quite "butter fingers", but soooooo close!

- Food was also the culprit in 2021, when Swedish player Rami Kaib broke his jaw eating a carrot. Advice? Cook it next time, Rami!

- While at Leeds United, Rio Ferdinand suffered a muscle injury in his leg as a result of too much PlayStation action.

- Backup Queen of the South goalkeeper Sam Henderson was once tackled by a cow. Talk about a "calf injury".

- Hardman David Batty was taken out by his two-year-old daughter, who was riding a tricycle at the time.

NOW YOU'RE QUOTING...

Below is a famous footballing quote; it reads from left to right, then continues to the second row, and then to the third. We've intentionally left some letters out, and any punctuation has been omitted. Can you guess it?

	O		E	P			P			A		E
O		T		E	P			C	H		H	E
Y		H	I		K	I		S		L	L	O
	E	R	I		I	S	O					

METALLIC MEDALS

Since the 1982 World Cup, the Golden Ball award has been presented to the best player of every tournament. Runners-up have been given Silver and Bronze Ball accolades. Here's a low-down of the winners.

Year	Golden Ball winner	Silver Ball winner	Bronze Ball winner
1982	Paolo Rossi	Falcão	Karl-Heinz Rummenigge
1986	Diego Maradona	Harald Schumacher	Preben Elkjær
1990	Salvatore Schillaci	Lothar Matthäus	Diego Maradona
1994	Romário	Roberto Baggio	Hristo Stoichkov
1998	Ronaldo	Davor Šuker	Lilian Thuram
2002	Oliver Kahn	Ronaldo	Hong Myung-bo
2006	Zinedine Zidane	Fabio Cannavaro	Andrea Pirlo
2010	Diego Forlán	Wesley Sneijder	David Villa
2014	Lionel Messi	Thomas Müller	Arjen Robben
2018	Luka Modrić	Eden Hazard	Antoine Griezmann

WORLD CUP ONE-IN-THREE ?

Try your luck with three questions about the Four Lions' performances in World Cups. We've provided three answers for each question… but only one is correct. How well do you know the biggest footie tournament on Earth?

1. **Who is the only player for England to have scored in three World Cups?**
   a) David Platt
   b) Gary Lineker
   c) David Beckham

2. **Which defender scored twice in England's 6–1 victory over Panama in 2018?**
   a) Kieran Trippier
   b) John Stones
   c) Kyle Walker

3. **At the 2014 World Cup in Brazil, in which position did England finish when all the group matches had been played (four teams in each group)?**
   a) second place (advanced to knockout stage)
   b) third place (knocked out)
   c) fourth place (knocked out)

HITTING THE HIGH NOTE?

Some people just shouldn't be allowed to sing – check out your local pub on karaoke night for the evidence! However, someone should tell that to certain footballers over the years. In 2003, Channel 4 asked viewers to vote for the worst singles of all time. Three songs in this most undesirable of lists were by footballers. Which ones?

1. "Back Home" by the 1970 England World Cup squad. Talented players, terrible song.

2. "Fog on the Tyne" by Paul Gascoigne. He loves Newcastle, but our ears apparently hated that song. Sorry, Gazza!

3. "Diamond Lights" by Glenn Hoddle and Chris Waddle. Both were mulleted midfield maestros, but both proved atrocious in front of the microphone.

PICTURE PERFECT

Below are some words and pictures that, when combined, make up the first names and surnames of footballers who have scored at World Cups.

1. **Goliath slayer +**

2. **Houdini +**

3. **Garden +**

2022 FIFA RANKINGS

At the end of March 2022, FIFA published their rankings for national men's footie teams.

Ranking	Team
1	Brazil
2	Belgium
3	France
4	Argentina
5	England
6	Italy
7	Spain
8	Portugal
9	Mexico
10	Netherlands
11	Denmark
12	Germany
13	Uruguay
14	Switzerland
15	USA
16	Croatia
17	Colombia
18	Wales
19	Sweden
20	Senegal

And in the last spot (no. 211) on FIFA's list? That'll be San Marino!

GENERALLY SPEAKING

Here are some general quiz questions that'll appeal to fans who like to grill their friends!

1. The name of which European club consists of 11 letters – with *every other* letter being an "a"?

2. Who was the only member of England's Euro 1996 squad that didn't play for a UK team at the time?

3. Who started as goalkeeper for Arsenal at their last game at Highbury, and at their first game at the Emirates?

4. Which Spanish city hosted games at Euro 2020?

5. Mbwana Samatta was the first player from his country to score in the Premier League. In which country was he born?

The trend for World Cup mascots began in 1966. Take a look at those that followed in England's footsteps.

Year	Host	Mascot	Description
1966	England	Willie	Lion in a Union Jack jersey
1970	Mexico	Juanito	Mexican boy wearing a sombrero
1974	West Germany	Tip and Tap	Two boys wearing German kits
1978	Argentina	Gauchito	Boy in Argentine kit, with a whip, hat and neckerchief
1982	Spain	Naranjito	Orange (as in the fruit) wearing the Spanish kit
1986	Mexico	Pique	Moustachioed jalapeño pepper wearing a sombrero
1990	Italy	Ciao	Italian Tricolore stick figure with a football head
1994	USA	Striker	Smiling dog in USA colours
1998	France	Footix	Cockerel holding a ball
2002	Japan and South Korea	Ato, Kaz and Nik	Orange, purple and blue computer-generated humanoid creatures

Year	Host	Mascot	Description
2006	Germany	Goleo VI and Pille	Lion wearing a Germany shirt and a talking football
2010	South Africa	Zakumi	Green-haired leopard
2014	Brazil	Fuleco	Three-banded armadillo
2018	Russia	Zabivaka	Wolf whose name means "the Goal Scorer" in Russian
2022	Qatar	La'eeb	Translated as "skilful player" from Arabic

YOU'RE IN CHARGE!

If you were the referee, would you know the correct answers to these five puzzling events below? They are all in the FA rulebook, and we'll give you a 50:50 chance on all of them!

1. Before the game starts, you notice the ball looks a little deflated. What is the correct circumference of a football for an adult game?

   a) 27–28 inches

   b) 29–30 inches

2. During the coin toss before the start of the game, the United captain spits at the Rovers captain. What course of action do you take?

   a) Send the United captain off, with no substitute allowed to take his place

   b) Send the United captain off, but allow a named substitute to take his place

3. It's a chilly day, and one of the goalkeepers is wearing a pair of tracksuit bottoms. Do you allow him to wear these "leg warmers", or insist he wears shorts?

   a) Yes, tracksuit bottoms are allowed for goalies

   b) No – he must take them off and don his shorts

4. A match may not start or continue if either team has fewer than how many players?
   a) Seven
   b) Eight

5. When you've awarded a corner kick, what is the minimum distance an opponent must remain from the corner arc, until the ball is in play?
   a) 5 yards
   b) 10 yards

MISSING LETTER

Each of the following football-related words is missing a letter. Put the seven missing letters into the grid below to spell out a word familiar to English football fans.

1. S_EEPER
2. SOCC_R
3. _IDFIELD
4. TRE_LE
5. _OAN
6. FRI_NDLY
7. VOLLE_

1	2	3	4	5	6	7

FOURFOURTWO LEGENDS

Published in 2021, cult footie website *FourFourTwo* ranked the top 100 best footballers to appear in the Premier League (it's their opinion, but they know what they're talking about!). There isn't enough space for the full list, but here is their top ten. Their rankings are based on each player's impact: a combination of ability, status and special moments on the pitch. To crank up the suspense, let's reveal the top ten in descending order.

10. Paul Scholes

9. Patrick Vieira

8. Frank Lampard

7. Steven Gerrard

6. Eric Cantona

5. Ryan Giggs

4. Wayne Rooney

3. Alan Shearer

2. Cristiano Ronaldo

1. Thierry Henry

BRAZILIAN FLAIR

?

Here's a "top ten" question that'll leave some fans bamboozled.

The question: Can you name the ten Brazilian footballers that had five or more goals and assists (combined) in the 2019-2020 Premier League season?

1. _____

2. _____

3. _____

4. _____

5. _____

6. _____

7. _____

8. _____

9. _____

10. _____

Every year, FIFA grants the Puskás Award to "the player judged to have scored the most aesthetically significant goal, regardless of championship, gender or nationality, and scored without the result of luck or a mistake and in support of fair play". In short, it's the most beautiful goal of the year and is named after the Hungarian legend Ferenc Puskás.

As of March 2022, Lionel Messi has been nominated seven times, Neymar five times and Zlatan Ibrahimović four times.

The 2021 award went to Erik Lamela's *rabona* goal for Spurs against Arsenal. *Rabona* is the technique of striking a ball where the kicking leg is crossed behind the back of the standing leg. The word means "skipping school" in Spanish.

Below are the other winners prior to Lamela's genius touch. You might be able to find videos of these crackers online.

2020 – Son Heung-min, Spurs v Burnley
2019 – Daniel Zsóri, Debrecen v Ferencváros
2018 – Mohamed Salah, Liverpool v Everton
2017 – Olivier Giroud, Arsenal v Crystal Palace
2016 – Mohd Faiz Subri, Penang v Pahang
2015 – Wendell Lira, Goianésia v Atlético Goianiense

BRAZILIAN GRID

We've hidden the names of four Brazilian World Cup stars – either past or present – in the grid below. The names can be found by moving one letter at a time, either vertically or horizontally. What are the four names?

A	L	F	W	E	D	I
C	K	O	F	R	M	I
K	M	N	A	D	L	N
A	K	Q	C	G	H	E
W	A	U	A	F	R	Z
C	P	E	L	U	S	I
C	F	U	P	H	O	C

THERE'S NO PLACE LIKE HOME

Without stadiums (or should that be "stadia"?), football matches with wider audiences just wouldn't happen. Whether you're a season ticket holder or just a casual spectator, here are a few stats about stadiums around the world.

- "Stadium" was originally a Latin unit of length roughly equal to an eighth of a mile.

- According to *The Daily Express*, Wembley Stadium's volume of 4 million m^3 would take 7 billion pints of fluid to fill it!

According to the most prominent website on football stadiums, here are the "Best Football Stadiums to Visit":

- **Camp Nou (Barcelona)**

- **Anfield (Liverpool)**

- **Old Trafford (Manchester United)**

- **San Siro (Milan teams)**

- **Maracanã (Rio de Janeiro)**

NORTH LONDON STARTING LINE-UPS

Here are two teasers for North London fans.

The two teams below were the starting XIs for José Mourinho's and Arsène Wenger's first games in charge (in 2019 for Spurs and 1996 for Arsenal, respectively). Which four players are missing from the team sheets?

Spurs	Arsenal
Gazzaniga	Seaman
Aurier	Dixon
Alderweireld	Adams
Sanchez	Bould
Davies	?
?	Winterburn
?	Merson
Dele	Platt
Lucas	Vieira
Son	Hartson
Kane	?

While Pelé is so famous he doesn't need an introduction, let's at least share some interesting facts about the man nicknamed "Dico".

- Pelé was born Edson Arantes do Nascimento on 23 October 1940 in Minas Gerais, a state in south-east Brazil.

- One of his sons, Edinho, is a coach and former goalkeeper.

- Pelé played for the Brazilian national team from 1957 to 1971.

- In November 1969, Pelé scored his 1,000th goal in his 909th first-class match.

- Pelé was known as "Pérola Negra", translated as "Black Pearl".

- After retiring from football in 1977, Pelé used his fame to work with good causes; in 1994, he was appointed a UNESCO Goodwill Ambassador.

- As of May 2022, Pelé had 8.8 million followers on Instagram – that's roughly the population of Switzerland!

- Speaking of Instagram, Pelé's introduction on his account states: "Brazilian #10, 3x World Cup Champion, Leading Goal Scorer of All Time (1,283[*]), FIFA Football Player of the Century, Global Ambassador and Humanitarian".

[*] This includes friendlies, as FIFA recognizes Cristiano Ronaldo as the leading goalscorer in "official" matches.

CROSS OUT

Cross out the letters in the grid below that appear more than once. With the remaining letters, find the surname of a footballer who was the joint top goalscorer in a World Cup.

S	N	P	E	I
H	B	R	U	D
A	W	U	C	O
T	D	T	K	H
K	L	S	W	E
B	C	I	P	F

WORLD CUP 2018 TOP GOALSCORERS

The 2018 Russia World Cup will always be remembered for England's semi-final run, among other things. But can you recall who the top scorers were that year? There's no need because here they are!

No. of goals	Player
6	Harry Kane
4	Romelu Lukaku Antoine Griezmann Kylian Mbappé Cristiano Ronaldo Denis Cheryshev
3	Eden Hazard Yerry Mina Mario Mandžukić Ivan Perišić Artem Dzyuba Diego Costa Edinson Cavani

WHO SAID THAT?

Below are some quotes attributed to footballers or managers. Can you identify who said them? You'll have a one-in-three chance.

1. "Some people believe football is a matter of life and death. I'm very disappointed with that attitude. I can assure you it is much, much more important than that."

   a) Brian Clough

   b) Bill Nicholson

   c) Bill Shankly

2. "A penalty is a cowardly way to score."

   a) Michel Platini

   b) Pelé

   c) Lionel Messi

3. "One accusation you can't throw at me is that I've always done my best."

   a) Michael Owen

   b) Alan Shearer

   c) Robbie Fowler

4. "I couldn't be more chuffed if I were a badger at the start of the mating season!"
   a) Ian Holloway
   b) Neil Warnock
   c) Roy Hodgson

5. "You'll never win anything with kids."
   a) Graeme Souness
   b) Kenny Dalglish
   c) Alan Hansen

FanChants is the no. 1 online archive for football chants and the leading authority on footie songs. The website has collated over 20,000 chants submitted by fans all over the world. Below is a table of the Premier League football teams with the most songs. The songs are categorized as the following:

A – Anthems
C – Classic
F – Funny
H – Hall of Fame (songs about fans' favourite players)
G – 'Aving a go (riling rival teams)
V – Vintage

Let's find out which teams' fans have the most songs… "'Ere we go, 'ere we go, 'ere we go!"

Football team	Total no. songs
Manchester United	551
Newcastle United	513
Leeds United	427
Arsenal	424

Football team	Total no. songs
Chelsea	374
Wolves	294
Liverpool	268
Manchester City	255
Spurs	219
Aston Villa	210
West Ham United	190
Everton	149
Leicester City	146
Crystal Palace	143
Brighton	139
Watford	121
Southampton	117
Norwich	116
Brentford	112
Burnley	92

WORD SEARCH – FINDING "THE INVINCIBLES"

The 2003–2004 season led to the Arsenal squad being labelled "the Invincibles" after 49 undefeated games. Find the following 11 players below – the most used in that season.

Lehman, Touré, Campbell, Cole, Lauren, Vieira, Gilberto, Pires, Ljungberg, Bergkamp, Henry,

C	O	L	E	O	L	E	H	M	A	N
A	Q	W	E	R	T	Y	U	I	O	P
M	A	S	D	F	G	H	J	K	L	T
P	Z	X	C	V	B	N	M	Q	Q	O
B	W	E	R	V	T	T	Y	U	I	U
E	A	S	P	I	R	E	S	S	D	R
L	A	U	R	E	N	F	G	H	J	É
L	O	P	G	I	L	B	E	R	T	O
Z	X	B	E	R	G	K	A	M	P	C
V	B	N	M	A	Q	E	R	T	Y	U
Z	Z	B	B	N	M	H	E	N	R	Y
L	J	U	N	G	B	E	R	G	K	L

ENGLISH CLUBS AT THE WORLD CUP

To any English fan, it doesn't matter which local team you support when England are in the World Cup. But you get extra bragging rights if you support the following clubs who have sent the most players to World Cup finals from 1950 to 2018.

Club	No. players represented
Manchester United	99
Liverpool	78
Chelsea	77
Arsenal	74
Tottenham Hotspur	73
Manchester City	53
Everton	40
Aston Villa	31
Leeds United	30
West Ham United	29

WHO AM I?

Here are some more names to identify from brief facts.

1. I won the Ballon d'Or in 2001. I scored 40 goals for my country, and I played in England and Spain during my senior career.

2. I was a Brazilian attacking midfielder and striker with the surname "Ferreira", although like some of my teammates, I'm better known by one word. I've played in several countries in my senior career, including Brazil, Italy, Spain, Greece, Angola and Uzbekistan.

3. I was born in Essex and, as caretaker manager for England, I made David Beckham national captain for the first time.

4. I was born in 1980 and played for just two clubs in my senior career. I am the only player for the club I'm most associated with to feature in the club's all-time top five for both appearances and goals. I was quoted as saying, "Cut my veins open and I bleed [club's name] red."

5. A one-club player, I am nicknamed "Mr Arsenal".

REMOTELY SPEAKING

Ever fancied attending a footie match where no one knows your name? Well, try these three pitches out for size – they are among the most remote on Earth.

1. Galolhu Rasmee Dhandu Stadium – Malé, Maldives
Located in the Maldives' capital, this is the national stadium and holds around 11,000 spectators – about 8 per cent of Malé's population. The stadium is just under 500 miles from Sri Lanka!

2. Henningsvær Stadion – Lofoten, Norway
With a lack of proper seating, this pitch is located on a rocky islet in north-west Norway. Large metal racks border the pitch to prevent the ball ending up in the surrounding water. The same racks are also used to dry cod! Though one of the most spectacular footie destinations out there, avoid it if you need to catch a bus back home.

3. The Floating Pitch – Koh Panyee, Thailand
Floating on stilts, this is a major tourist attraction. Potential for lost balls is high!

ODD ONE OUT ANAGRAM

Which one of the following anagrams is the anomaly? They all relate to football managers or coaches.

1. COLLAPE
2. PILLGREENI
3. HUMIORON
4. NARRIIE
5. TEBZINE

BEST TEAM IN THE WORLD IN 2018?

After the World Cup in Russia, FIFA conducted a poll of their website users to come up with their own 2018 World Cup dream team, and to see if they could select the same line-up as FIFA. Here is FIFA's from the Russian tournament.

Position	Player	% of users who voted for the player
Goalkeeper	Thibaut Courtois	19.0
Defender	Diego Godin	25.8
Defender	Marcelo	18.0
Defender	Thiago Silva	29.3
Defender	Raphaël Varane	31.5
Midfielder	Philippe Coutinho	45.6
Midfielder	Kevin De Bruyne	30.6
Midfielder	Luka Modrić	49.0
Striker	Harry Kane	36.3
Striker	Kylian Mbappé	41.1
Striker	Cristiano Ronaldo	25.2

COLOURFUL NATIONAL FLAGS

Since you're a fan of the beautiful game, these questions might be easy... but who knows?

Can you name the *main* colours of the following nations? Geographical knowledge will help (of course), but footie fans will surely have seen the flags numerous times on screen. The number of colours on each flag is in brackets.

1. **Croatia (3)**

2. **Peru (2)**

3. **Cameroon (3)**

4. **Colombia (3)**

5. **South Africa (6 in total)**

Kevin Keegan is as much renowned for his spoken gaffes as his football and management abilities. Here are some absolute belters from the South Yorkshire legend.

"The thirty-three or thirty-four-year-olds will be thirty-six or thirty-seven by the time the next World Cup comes around, if they're not careful."

"Argentina won't be at Euro 2000 – because they're from South America."

"Even though two and two might look like four, it could be three or five."

"In some ways, cramp is worse than having a broken leg."

"I'm not disappointed – just disappointed."

"I came to Nantes two years ago and it's much the same today, except that it's totally different."

"The substitute is about to come on – he's a player who was left out of the starting line-up today."

"The Germans only have one player under twenty-two, and he's twenty-three!"

"They're the second-best team in the world, and there's no higher praise than that!"

"Luís Figo is totally different to David Beckham, and vice versa."

"Hungary is very similar to Bulgaria. I know they're different countries…"

King Kev, take a bow!

HIDDEN LADY

Starting with any letter, but going from letter to letter either vertically or horizontally, try to find the name of a notable female footballer. By way of a clue, the first letters of the player's given name and surname are highlighted in bold.

L	I	**B**	S	A	E	R
E	D	J	**B**	Y	C	O
N	F	O	R	V	U	W
A	Z	N	I	K	L	C
Q	E	G	E	N	E	C
U	P	A	U	L	E	S
I	F	E	O	E	H	O

THOSE IN CHARGE OF "BRINGING IT HOME"

All English fans hope the World Cup trophy is indeed "coming home", and one of the most important people in achieving this is the manager. Here are all the England managers. How many can you remember?

Manager	Dates in charge	No. of matches
Gareth Southgate	2016-present	70*
Sam Allardyce	2016	1
Roy Hodgson	2012-2016	56
Stuart Pearce	2012	1
Fabio Capello	2008-2011	42
Steve McClaren	2006-2007	18
Sven-Göran Eriksson	2001-2006	67
Peter Taylor	2000	1
Kevin Keegan	1999-2000	18
Howard Wilkinson	1999-2000	2

Manager	Dates in charge	No. of matches
Glenn Hoddle	1996–1998	28
Terry Venables	1994–1996	24
Graham Taylor	1990–1993	38
Bobby Robson	1982–1990	95
Ron Greenwood	1977–1982	55
Don Revie	1974–1977	29
Joe Mercer	1974	7
Alf Ramsey	1963–1974	113
Walter Winterbottom	1946–1962	139
[Committee]	[1872–1939]	[226]

* Up to May 2022.

SO... NOW YOU KNOW

?

The world of sport often reveals bizarre truths, and football is certainly no exception. See how you get on with the following questions – some of which could make you a legend at your own local club or down at the pub!

1. In 1999, which unusual clause did Sunderland FC put into Swedish footballer Stefan Schwarz's contract that prevented him from achieving a pretty weird lifetime ambition?

2. In 2018, which former Chelsea manager pulled out of the fourth stage of the Dakar Rally after crashing into a sand dune and injuring his back?

3. Instead of buying or renting an apartment during his time as Manchester United manager, José Mourinho stayed at which hotel in Salford, about two miles from Old Trafford?

4. What links Cristiano Ronaldo with something that is "approximately" 13 billion years old?

5. In 1994, West Ham United (managed by Harry Redknapp) played Oxford City in a pre-season friendly. Steve Davies for "the Hammers" scored; why was this unusual?

WHAT WERE THE ODDS?

Here's a little bit of local footie trivia that will appeal to players, fans and bookies alike.

Picture the scene: On a typical Saturday in January 2001, Worthing and Bromley went head-to-head in a Ryman League match. Players were itching to impress, and the spectators were anticipating an exciting match. What they couldn't predict was a bizarre incident in the sixty-third minute.

Two players with exactly the same name, playing for different teams, were both shown red cards following the same incident!

That's right – Danny Smith from Bromley and Danny Smith from Worthing both saw red after referee Mr Overall, according to spectators, "lost the plot".

Graham Sharpe, from bookmakers William Hill (and an expert on quirky footie facts), said he had never heard anything like it before. He estimated the odds would be around 10,000:1.

Eight other players were also booked, and the match ended in a 2–2 draw.

WORD LADDER

Change one letter at a time to reveal a famous four-letter surname found "between the sticks".

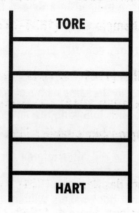

TORE

HART

ENGLAND IN ALL COMPS

Starting with the earliest participation at the top, here is a list of all competitions the England national football team has played in.

- Friendly (1872–March 2022), 396 matches

- British Home Championship (1884–1984), 254 matches

- World Cup qualifier (1949–2021), 122 matches

- World Cup finals (1950–2018), 69 matches

- European Championship qualifier (1962–2019), 108 matches

- Nations' Cup (Taça das Nações) (1964), 3 matches

- European Championship finals (1968–2021), 38 matches

- US Bicentennial Cup Tournament (1976), 2 matches

- Ciudad de México Cup (1985), 2 matches

- Azteca 2000 Tournament (1985), 1 match

- Rous Cup (1985–1989), 8 matches

- England Challenge Cup (1991), 2 matches

- United States Cup (1993), 3 matches
- Umbro International Trophy (1995), 3 matches
- Tournoi de France (1997), 3 matches
- King Hassan II Tournament (1998), 2 matches
- FA Summer Tournament (2004), 2 matches
- UEFA Nations League (2018–2020), 12 matches

ONE FOR THE YOUNGER FANS

Football is enjoyed by people of all ages around the world, so let's not forget about younger fans. Here are five teasers sure to tickle the more youthful funny bone!

1. Why did the football coach buy bibs for all the players?

2. What do you call it when a T-Rex achieves a hat trick?

3. What is a striker's favourite drink to order in a café?

4. Why doesn't Cinderella make a good goalkeeper?

5. Why was it so windy on the football pitch?

ANSWERS

PAGE 6 – ANAGRAM SCRAMBLE
Free kick
Dribble
Offside
Corner
Crossbar

PAGE 9 – STRANGE BUT TRUE
2. Because the laws dictate that players can't leave the field of play until the match ends, Goycochea needed to "relieve" himself on the pitch prior to the penalty shoot-out in the 1990 World Cup quarter-finals against Yugoslavia. Argentina won, so the goalie repeated the ritual before every shoot-out until he retired in 1998.

PAGE 11 – WORD LADDER
One possible solution: PUNT, PINT, MINT, MINE, MANE, KANE

PAGE 13 – CAPTAIN FANTASTICS
1. Germany's Philipp Lahm
2. Bobby Moore (An additional fact is that, even though he was well-known for playing for West Ham United, one of his middle names was also the name of their rival club, "Chelsea".)
3. Italy's Dino Zoff
4. France's Hugo Lloris
5. Dunga

PAGE 16 – VOWEL YOU'RE TALKING!
DVDBCKHM **David Beckham**

ZC **Zico**

LK MDRC **Luka Modrić**

NDRS NST **Andrés Iniesta**

SML T **Samuel Eto'o**

PL **Pelé**

NYMR **Neymar**

LN SHRR **Alan Shearer**

PL MLDN **Paolo Maldini**

PAGE 18 - FOOTIE RIDDLES

Footballer 1 – Stuart Pearce (stew-art pierce)
Footballer 2 – Tony Adams (toe-knee Adams)

PAGE 20 - FOOTIE TEASERS

1. 8 ft (2.4 m)
2. Due to being the only club to have won the FA Cup three years in a row, they are allowed to depict their club crest on their corner flags.
3. 114,000 (it opened on 1 May 1989)
4. Leicester City
5. Brian Deane for Sheffield United

PAGE 22 - WORD SEARCH

J	E	R	S	E	Y	Z	S	Z	T	W
A	T	Y	U	U	O	O	H	N	R	A
B	S	T	R	E	A	N	O	N	A	T
V	O	Q	W	E	R	T	R	P	N	E
W	P	O	A	T	T	E	T	H	S	R
S	O	O	T	Y	B	I	S	Y	F	B
O	A	A	C	S	W	E	R	S	E	O
C	A	S	H	K	L	E	S	I	R	T
K	O	A	G	E	N	T	I	O	X	T
S	X	B	M	W	M	K	I	I	P	L
Q	M	A	N	A	G	E	R	J	J	E
V	P	R	O	M	O	T	I	O	N	L

135

PAGE 24 – FAIR PLAY OR FIBBING?
1. True
2. True
3. False – it was "only" 26.3 billion
4. False – he scored 13 goals (still a record, though!)
5. True, with 99 players provided

PAGE 27 – FOOTIE TEAMS WORD JIG
Barcelona, Bayern Munich, Boca Juniors, Sampdoria, Marseille

PAGE 29 – FROM ONE TO TEN
1. Eight. Brazil (5); Italy and Germany (4); Uruguay, Argentina and current champion, France (2); England and Spain (1)
2. Six (1986)
3. Three (Arsenal, Aston Villa, Everton)
4. One
5. Two (Japan and South Korea)
6. Nine
7. Four
8. Ten
9. Seven
10. Five

PAGE 31 – ODD ONE OUT ANAGRAM
3. NOOLAS – Anagram of a Spanish footballer (Alonso).
The others are German: Kroos, Klose, Ozil and Werner

PAGE 33 – FOOTBALLING ALIASES
1. Franz Beckenbauer
2. Fernando Torres
3. Javier Hernández
4. Sergio Agüero
5. Fitz Hall (geddit?!)
6. Duncan Ferguson
7. Emlyn Hughes
8. Diego Maradona
9. Stuart Pearce
10. David Beckham

PAGE 36 – FOOTBALLING LETTERBOX
RAUL

PAGE 38 – STRANGE BUT TRUE
4. Infiltrating the Manchester United line-up before the team's match against Bayern Munich – as a prankster, not an official player.

PAGE 41 – FOLLOW THE LETTERS
Buffon, Neymar, Ramos, Salah

PAGE 43 – WHAT'S THAT SOUND?

1	2	3	4	5	6	7
W	H	I	S	T	L	E

PAGE 45 – WHO'S THE BOSS?
Ancelotti, Guardiola, Conte, Mourinho, Wenger

PAGE 47 – WORLD CUP RECALL
1. Peter Beardsley, Peter Reid, Terry Fenwick, Peter Shilton
2. Lothar Matthäus (4), Andreas Brehme, Rudi Völler and Jürgen Klinsmann (3 each)
3. Rose Bowl, Pasadena, California

PAGE 50 – RIDDLE ME THIS...
Football team no. 1 = Queens Park Rangers
Football team no. 2 = Forest Green Rovers

PAGE 53 – WHO AM I?
1. Michael Ballack

2. David Platt

PAGE 55 – AMUSING ANAGRAMS
Juan Mata, Diego Maradona, David Ginola, Fabrizio Ravanelli, Edwin van der Sar

1. True (in 1985)
2. True
3. False – it was "only" £80 million.
4. False – he was joint top scorer, with five goals.
5. True – in his native Madeira.
6. True
7. False – he was referring to children, not football.
8. False – it was 2018.

PAGE 60 – WORD SEARCH

E	A	G	L	E	S	V	W	E	R	B
Q	F	O	X	E	S	I	G	S	S	L
T	D	C	H	H	P	L	U	O	E	U
O	X	L	N	K	A	L	N	R	A	E
F	O	A	S	S	T	A	N	E	G	S
F	G	R	J	L	K	I	E	D	U	E
E	I	E	I	R	R	N	R	D	L	G
E	O	T	E	Q	H	S	S	E	L	C
S	G	S	A	W	X	K	E	V	S	V
E	G	P	C	A	N	A	R	I	E	S
H	A	M	M	E	R	S	K	L	K	M
M	A	G	P	I	E	S	L	S	E	N

PAGE 63 – 1962 – WHAT HAPPENED NEXT?

3. The dog was confronted by Jimmy Greaves, resulting in the canine "relieving" itself over the England striker's shirt – literally causing a stink!

PAGE 65 - PUZZLING FOOTBALL TEAMS
1. Basildon United (Basil, Don, united)
2. Charlton Athletic (Charlton, athletic)
3. Swansea City (Swan, sea, city)

PAGE 67 - JUMBLED-UP SURNAMES
Gascoigne, Bergkamp, Platini, Baggio

PAGE 69 - FOOTBALLING ANAGRAMS
1. John Terry
2. Rio Ferdinand
3. Teddy Sheringham
4. John Barnes
5. Chris Waddle

PAGE 71 - FIFA ALL-STAR XI
Lev Yashin, Paolo Maldini, Franz Beckenbauer, Roberto Carlos, Roberto Baggio, Zinedine Zidane (you all should have got that!), Michel Platini, Diego Maradona, Romário, Johan Cruyff, Pelé

PAGE 73 - UTTERLY QUOTABLE
SQUEAKY BUM TIME (attributed to Sir Alex Ferguson)

PAGE 76 - MANAGER'S SPECIAL
Arsenal - Ozil
Manchester United - Herrera

PAGE 78 - WORD LADDER
One possible solution: SALT, SALE, SAME, SOME, ROME, ROMA

PAGE 80 - REFEREES IN THE SPOTLIGHT
1. b) Having complained of back pain, Shmolik was moving erratically throughout the game - especially the second half. After the match, tests proved that Mr Shmolik was, in fact, incredibly drunk.
2. b) The English ref showed the same player a yellow card three times.

PAGE 83 – GLOBAL JUMBLE
1. Boca Juniors, 2. Inter Milan, 3. Kaizer Chiefs, 4. Villarreal, 5. Galatasaray

PAGE 85 – GLOBAL TEAMS
Corinthians – São Paulo, River Plate – Buenos Aires, Al Ahly SC – Cairo
Forge FC – Hamilton, The Strongest – La Paz, FK Partizan – Belgrade
AIK – Stockholm, Young Boys – Bern, Beşiktaş – Istanbul, HIFK – Helsinki
Bohemians Praha 1905 – Prague, América – Mexico City

PAGE 87 – ENGLAND WORLD CUP JIG
Lineker, Charlton, Greaves, Shilton, Moore

PAGE 89 – THE RIDDLER STRIKES AGAIN!
Dave predicted the score would be 0-0 before the game starts, and he was correct: the score is always "0-0" before any game starts (except for second legs!)

PAGE 92 – NOW YOU'RE QUOTING!
"Some people are on the pitch... they think it's all over... it is now."

PAGE 94 – WORLD CUP ONE-IN-THREE
1. c)   David Beckham (1998, 2002, 2006)
2. b)   John Stones
3. c)   Fourth (last) place

PAGE 96 – PICTURE PERFECT
1. David Villa
2. Harry Kane
3. Eden Hazard

PAGE 98 – GENERALLY SPEAKING
1. Galatasaray
2. Paul Ince (Inter Milan)
3. Jens Lehman
4. Seville
5. Tanzania

PAGE 101 – YOU'RE IN CHARGE!

1. a, 2. b, 3. a, 4. a, 5. b

PAGE 103 – MISSING LETTER

1	2	3	4	5	6	7
W	E	M	B	L	E	Y

PAGE 105 – BRAZILIAN FLAIR

Gabriel Jesus (Manchester City, 12 goals and 7 assists)
Richarlison (Everton, 13 goals and 3 assists)
Willian (Chelsea, 9 goals and 7 assists)
Roberto Firmino (Liverpool, 8 goals and 7 assists)
Lucas Moura (Tottenham Hotspur, 4 goals and 4 assists)
Wesley (Aston Villa, 5 goals and 1 assist)
Bernard (Everton, 3 goals and 2 assists)
Douglas Luiz (Aston Villa, 3 goals and 2 assists)
Fabinho (Liverpool, 2 goals and 3 assists)
Felipe Anderson (West Ham United, 1 goal and 4 assists)

PAGE 107 – BRAZILIAN GRID

Kaka, Fred, Cafu, Zico

A	L	F	W	E	D	I
C	K	O	F	R	M	I
K	M	N	A	D	L	N
A	K	Q	C	G	H	E
W	A	U	A	F	R	Z
C	P	E	L	U	S	I
C	F	U	P	H	O	C

PAGE 109 – NORTH LONDON STARTING LINE-UPS

Spurs – Dier and Winks

Arsenal – Keown and Wright

PAGE 111 – CROSS OUT

Forlán

PAGE 113 – WHO SAID THAT?

1. c) Bill Shankly
2. b) Pelé
3. b) Alan Shearer
4. a) Ian Holloway
5. c) Alan Hansen

PAGE 117 – WORD SEARCH: FINDING THE "INVINCIBLES"

C	O	L	E	O	L	E	H	M	A	N
A	Q	W	E	R	T	Y	U	I	O	P
M	A	S	D	F	G	H	J	K	L	T
P	Z	X	C	V	B	N	M	Q	Q	O
B	W	E	R	V	T	T	Y	U	I	U
E	A	S	P	I	R	E	S	S	D	R
L	A	U	R	E	N	F	G	H	J	É
L	O	P	G	I	L	B	E	R	T	O
Z	X	B	E	R	G	K	A	M	P	C
V	B	N	M	A	Q	E	R	T	Y	U
Z	Z	B	B	N	M	H	E	N	R	Y
L	J	U	N	G	B	E	R	G	K	L

PAGE 119 – WHO AM I?
1. Michael Owen
2. Rivaldo
3. Peter Taylor
4. Steven Gerrard
5. Tony Adams

PAGE 121 – ODD ONE OUT ANAGRAM
4 – RANIERI. The others have managed or been head coach of Real Madrid (CAPELLO, PELLEGRINI, MOURINHO, BENITEZ)

PAGE 123 – COLOURFUL NATIONAL FLAGS
1. Red, white, blue. 2. Red, white. 3. Green, red, yellow. 4. Yellow, blue, red. 5. Red, white, green, blue, yellow, black

PAGE 125 – HIDDEN LADY
LUCY BRONZE

PAGE 128 – SO... NOW YOU KNOW
1. Sunderland inserted a "Space Clause" into his contract, meaning if the intrepid midfielder travelled into space, his contract would become invalid.
2. André Villas-Boas.
3. The Lowry (in one of six Riverside suites, starting at £600 per night).
4. The Cosmos Redshift 7 galaxy – CR7 for short. The name was inspired by Ronaldo.
5. Davies was a fan in the crowd, and Redknapp "asked" him if he could do any better than the current centre forward Lee Chapman, who Davies was saying wasn't performing well. Davies duly complied after Redknapp asked him, "Can you play as good as you can talk?"

PAGE 130 – WORD LADDER
One possible solution: TORE, TIRE, DIRE, DIRT, DART, HART

PAGE 133 – ONE FOR THE YOUNGER FANS
1. Because they kept dribbling!
2. A dino-score!
3. A cup of penal-tea!
4. Because she always runs away from the ball!
5. Because there were so many fans in the stadium!

Have you enjoyed this book?

If so, why not write a review on your favourite website?

If you're interested in finding out more about our books,
find us on Facebook at **Summersdale Publishers**, on Twitter at
@Summersdale and on Instagram at **@summersdalebooks**
and get in touch. We'd love to hear from you!

Thanks very much for buying this Summersdale book.

www.summersdale.com